A YEAR OF FAMILY HOME EVENINGS

By
Karen Crossley
And
Roberta Hunter

Complete family home evening lessons with little to no preparation, using commonly found household items, and designed specifically for children ages three to ten. Excellent lessons for older children to teach to younger siblings.

Acknowledgments

We wish to acknowledge all the families who helped us test drive and fine tune these lessons. Thank you for your help. Everyone's input was very valuable and much appreciated.

Copyright © 2002 by Karen Crossley

All rights reserved.
Reproduction in whole or any part thereof, in any form or by any media, without written permission is prohibited.

A Year of Family Home Evenings
Artistic work by Valerie Winward

ISBN: 1-930980-81-5

Distributed by Granite Publishing
1-800-574-5779
Order #: 80817

Dedication

Dedicated to all the parents of young children who are valiantly struggling every day to be an Eternal Family. Love, enjoy, teach, and play with your children. They will remember it always.

Instructions/Advice

Be happy. Enjoy these lessons with your children. The lessons are important, but the most important thing is to spend time as a family. Build the tradition of family home evening as a fun yet learning time when the children are young.

Modify each lesson to suit your purposes. Omit or replace any part of the lesson that may be a stumbling block to you. For example: If you are not musically inclined, leave out the song or play a Primary music cassette or CD. Add to the lesson if so inspired. For example: Sing a closing song or ask more challenging questions of older children. We have been counseled by the prophets to have family home evening. However, they did not mandate the structure of the evening. Do what works for your family. The important thing is to have family home evening on a regular basis.

Give older children the opportunity to teach some of the lessons. Children listen to Mom and Dad all day long. It is a nice change of pace to be taught by a big brother or sister.

Some of these lessons involve going outside or refer to a specific season of the year. Watch for these lessons and plan appropriately. There are extra lessons that can be substituted until the weather clears up or the proper season rolls around.

Most importantly, enjoy the Gospel, love the Lord, and enjoy being a family.

Table of Contents

Lesson		Page
1.	The Prophet Says	1
2.	Nephi's Ship	2
3.	The Gift of the Scriptures	3
4.	Daniel in the Lions' Den	4
5.	Sense of Taste	5
6.	Habits	6
7.	72 Hour Kits	8
8.	Reenact Night	10
9.	Noah's Rainbow Promise	11
10.	Samuel the Lamanite	12
11.	Obedience	14
12.	Sense of Sight	15
13.	Manners	16
14.	Spring	17
15.	Modern Day Prophets	18
16.	Rocky Road	20
17.	Garden	21
18.	Make Our Homes a Safer Place	22
19.	Family Ten Commandments	24
20.	Listen to the Holy Ghost	25
21.	The Cornerstone	26
22.	King Benjamin's Tower	27
23.	Tithing	28
24.	Playdoh World	30
25.	Self Esteem	31
26.	Senses of Hearing and Smell	32
27.	Pioneers	34
28.	Play It Again, Sam	36
29.	The Burning Bush	37
30.	Our Bodies are a Wonderful Gift	38
31.	Feast Upon the Word	40
32.	Title of Liberty	41

33.	Emergency Preparedness	42
34.	Sense of Touch	43
35.	Autumn	44
36.	Tower of Babel	45
37.	I Can Be Quiet and Respectful in Church	46
38.	Line Upon Line	48
39.	God's Image	50
40.	Law of Sacrifice	51
41.	Feeding the Five Thousand	52
42.	Sacrament Reverence	53
43.	Service Spotlight	54
44.	David and Goliath	56
45.	The Liahona	58
46.	Noah's Ark	60
47.	Family Shield	62

Holiday Lessons:

48.	New Year Time Capsule	64
49.	Valentine's Day	65
50.	Easter	66
51.	Mother's/Father's Day	68
52.	4th of July	69
53.	Halloween	70
54.	Thanksgiving	71
55.	Christmas Gift	73
56.	Christmas Music	74

The Prophet Says

Purpose: Follow the Prophet.

Supplies: Scriptures

Opening Prayer

Song: Follow the Prophet   pg. 110 Children's Songbook

Activity: Begin by talking about our modern prophet. He is the leader of our church and he loves us very much. The prophet is a seer and revelator which means that Heavenly Father tells the prophet things that he wishes us to know and do, then the prophet tells us. Read 3 Nephi 23:5. The prophet has told us many things. If we are obedient to his counsel, we will be able to return to our Heavenly Father. Ask each family member to say something the prophets have instructed us to do. A few examples are: grow a garden, obtain a year's supply, genealogy work, attend the temple, pay tithing, keep the Sabbath holy.

To practice obeying the Prophet, play a variation of Simon Says. When the Prophet says to do something, do it. For example: when the Prophet says, "Jump up and down," do it. When the Prophet says, "Stand on one leg," do it. "Scratch your head," don't do it. Have everyone in the family take turns being the Prophet. Children will enjoy trying to trick the parents.

Closing Prayer

Quickly read the lesson for next week.

Nephi's Ship

Purpose: Reinforce that if we are obedient, the Lord will help us fulfill the tasks he has given us.

Supplies:
- Scriptures
- Corrugated cardboard
- Scissors
- Paper
- Toothpick

Opening Prayer

Song: Nephi's Courage   pg. 120 Children's Songbook

Activity: Begin by reading 1 Nephi 17:7-9. Nephi was instructed to build a ship. Remember that Nephi had grown up in a desert area. He had probably never seen a ship let alone know how to build one. Yet, he had faith and obeyed the Lord without question. Nephi broke the huge job of building a ship into manageable tasks and then went to work.

     Ore to make tools   1 Nephi 17:10

     Bellows and fire   1 Nephi 17:11

(Interesting point: up until this point in their journey no fire was required. The Lord made their food sweet without cooking [vs. 12], and he was their light in the wilderness [vs. 13].).

     Plans for the ship   1 Nephi 18:1-3

Heavenly Father has given us many tasks. He will give us many more. We need to obey Heavenly Father just as Nephi did, and he will help us too. Allow each family member to say something we should be doing to show our obedience to the Lord. A few examples are: reading the scriptures, attending our church meetings, saying our prayers, paying our tithing, loving our brothers & sisters, forgiving, etc.

Now for the fun! Take the cardboard and build a raft. Use the paper and toothpick to fashion a sail. If you are really creative, build a boat. Have family raft races in the bathtub!

Closing Prayer

Quickly read the lesson for next week.

The Gift of the Scriptures

Purpose: Help children understand that the scriptures are a gift from Heavenly Father.

Supplies: Scriptures
            Empty box
            Wrapping paper, scissors, tape

Advance Preparation: Wrap the scriptures in the box.

Opening Prayer

Song: Search, Ponder, and Pray   pg. 109 Children's Songbook

Activity: Place the wrapped box before the children. Explain that there is something wonderful inside. It is a gift from Heavenly Father. This gift will help us live so that we may return home to him. Give the children the chance to guess what is inside the box.

Unwrap the box and remove the scriptures. The scriptures are stories of our ancestors. Ancestors are people who lived a long time before us. The scriptures also guide us and let us know what Heavenly Father wants us to do. If we listen to his words, learn from the stories, and follow Jesus' example, we will be able to live with Heavenly Father again. Read D & C 33:16.

Give every family member the opportunity to share a favorite scripture or scripture story. Have them explain, if they can, why it is their favorite. What was learned? How did it make you want to change your life?

Closing Prayer

Quickly read the lesson for next week.

Daniel in the Lions' Den

Purpose: To show faith in all circumstances.

Supplies: Toy lions from the kids' toy box (if toy lions are not available draw some, make some from Playdoh, use other animals and your imagination).
Action figure from the kids' toy box
Pillows/cushions from couch or pillows from bed
Scriptures

Opening Prayer

Song: I Pray in Faith   pg. 14   Children's Songbook

Activity: Daniel was a very good man. He always tried to do what Heavenly Father asked. At the time Daniel lived, long ago, it was against the law to pray to Heavenly Father. However, Daniel was a good man and he knew that praying was the right thing to do. Read Daniel 6:10. Bad men took Daniel before the king to be punished for praying. According to the law, Daniel must be cast into the lions' den (vs. 12). The King and Daniel were friends and did not want to send Daniel to the lions but he had to uphold the law. The King believed Heavenly Father would protect Daniel (vs. 16). The next morning, the King rushed to the lions' den to release Daniel. Read 19-23. Daniel was saved because of his faith.

Now that you have read the story together, get out the lions and the action figure. Reenact the story with the children using the pillow/cushions to make the lions' den. Refer to the scriptures often and emphasize that Daniel had faith in the Lord. He said his prayers because he knew it was the right thing to do. Heavenly Father protected Daniel from the lions because of his faith.

We need to have faith like Daniel and never be afraid to do what we know is right.

Closing Prayer

Quickly read the lesson for next week.

Sense of Taste

Purpose: Increase appreciation for our sense of taste.

Supplies: Four paper cups (or similar containers)   Water
           Lemon Juice   Sugar
           Teaspoon for every family member   Vanilla flavoring
           Scriptures

Advance Preparation: Fill each paper cup one quarter full with water. To one cup add enough salt to make the water taste salty. To another cup add enough sugar to make the water taste sweet. Stir to dissolve. To the third cup, add enough lemon juice to make the water taste sour. Do likewise with the vanilla flavoring to make a bitter taste. Place all of the cups and the teaspoons together on the table.

Opening Prayer

Song: My Heavenly Father Loves Me   pg. 228 Children's Songbook

Activity: Heavenly Father has given us a wonderful world. We explore this world by using our senses. Our senses are: sight, sound, touch, smell and taste. Each sense helps us learn about our fantastic world. Learning is one of the things we have been put upon this earth to do.

Today we will talk about our sense of taste. Allow each person to name something that to him/her tastes absolutely delicious and another thing that to him/her tastes totally terrible. Everyone's likes and dislikes are different. This helps make us unique.

To demonstrate how wonderfully sensitive taste is, give everyone a teaspoon then have each person see if he/she can identify the taste (salty, sweet, sour, bitter).

Read D & C 59:18-19. Heavenly Father has given us a world full of things to see, taste, smell, touch and hear to strengthen our bodies and gladden our souls. Enjoy and be thankful for everything.

Closing Prayer   Quickly read the lesson for next week.

Habits

Purpose: To encourage us to break bad habits and replace them with good.

Supplies: Scriptures   Paper   Pencil/Pen

Opening Prayer

Song: Choose the Right Way   pg. 160   Children's Songbook

Activity: Today we are going to talk about habits. What is a habit? A habit is something that we do on a regular basis. It can be good or bad. Have each family member name a good and a bad habit. Examples of good habits are: praying daily, exercising daily, daily scripture study, being on time, always being positive, etc. Examples of bad habits are: telling fibs, talking back, being selfish and not sharing, using bad words, etc.

Good habits strengthen our bodies, minds, and spirits. Heavenly Father wants us to do those things which are good. Bad habits destroy our bodies and weaken our minds and spirits. Satan wants us to do these things which are bad. It takes only two times of doing something to develop a bad habit. Satan makes things so easy. On the other hand, it takes about thirty times of doing a good thing for it to become a good habit. Heavenly Father makes us work, but the reward will be great. Read Alma 3:26. We will be judged by our works/habits, and will be rewarded accordingly.

Pass pencil and paper to everyone. Younger children may need help writing. Have each family member determine a bad habit they would like to break. Write it down in the middle of their papers. The easiest way to break a bad habit is to replace it with a good one. Turn the paper over and write in nice large letters a good habit to start practicing every day. Place these papers where they can be seen every day as a reminder of their good habit goals. Each day that you work on your good habit (scripture study, home-work without fussing, exercise etc.) put a star on your paper.

Help and support each other in overcoming the bad habit. For example: if someone has a goal to no longer shout, when he/she starts to yell, give him/her a big hug and remind him/her to replace the bad habit with the new good habit.

In a month, meet again as a family and talk about your new good habits. Give family members the opportunity to talk about their experiences. They should be happy about their new good habits. Heavenly Father is pleased also and is aware of how hard everyone has been working.

Challenge: Maintain your good habit. Set a monthly goal to eliminate one bad habit by replacing it with a good one.

Closing Prayer

Quickly read the lesson for next week.

72 Hour Kits

Purpose: To familiarize the family with and update the items in the kits.

Supplies: 72 hour kits
               Scriptures

Opening Prayer

Song: If You're Happy   pg. 266 Children's Songbook

Activity: Read D&C 38:30. Heavenly Father has told us that if we are prepared we shall not fear. To help us be prepared, we have been encouraged to have 72 hour kits for everyone in the family in case of emergency. Begin the activity by showing the children where the kits are kept. Talk about different emergencies such as flood, fire, etc. that may require us to leave our homes. (Keep this part of the activity light-hearted.)

Have each family member go through his/her pack and verify that things are current. For example: If you wear glasses, make sure there is a pair of glasses with a reasonably current prescription in the kit. Make sure medications are in the kit and check their expiration date. If you have small children, make sure you have the right size diapers. Have everyone try on the clothes that are in their kits to verify they fit. Update the personal information, emergency addresses and phone numbers. Make sure the water containers aren't leaking. Change the batteries in the flashlights and emergency radio. Make sure that the food has not expired.

Get some hands on experience with some of your emergency supplies. Sit in a dark room and turn on your flashlights. Listen to your emergency radio and dine on some of your emergency rations. (Just be sure to replenish your supplies when you repack your kits.)

Emergencies are scary times but if we keep our kits current and keep a level head, we will be prepared for them. Remember: you need not fear if you are prepared.

Challenge: Learn some simple first aid techniques.

Closing Prayer   Quickly read the lesson for next week.

If you have any questions about 72 hour kits contact Price Enterprises, (208) 847-2274. They are very helpful, knowledgeable, and accommodating. They can answer questions or customize kits to your family's needs.

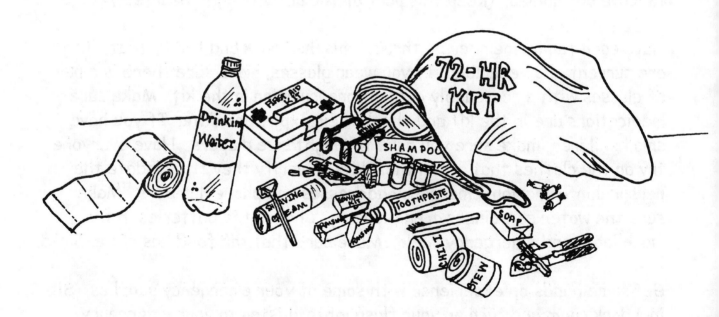

Reenact Night

Purpose: Allow the children to use their creativity to retell a favorite scripture story.

Supplies: Grab 6-7 miscellaneous items (scarf, wig, bracelet, jar lid, anything)
You may want to include the children. Let them gather several different things. Their imaginations will guide them.

Opening Prayer

Song: If You're Happy   pg. 266 Children's Songbook

Activity: This is an opportunity for the children to use their creativity. Encourage them to reenact one of their favorite scripture stories using the miscellaneous items as props. Place their selections in the middle of the floor. Give the children ten minutes to work out the details.

Parents, you may want to get involved by being in the play. Or if you'd rather you may sit on the sidelines, enjoy the show, and guess which story it is.

After the show, toss all the props back into the center of the room and let a different child share his/her favorite story. Continue the reenactments as along as the activity is enjoyable.

Closing Prayer

Quickly read the lesson for next week.

Noah's Rainbow Promise

Purpose: To teach the promise that the earth will never be flooded again. This is a simple lesson that could easily be taught by the older to the younger children. Parental help with the advance preparation is advised.

Supplies: Paper cups   Paper
            Q-tips   Scriptures
            Kool-Aid/Flavoraid (several different flavors/colors)

Advance Preparation: One paper cup for each flavor of Kool-Aid is needed. Cut two inches off the top of each cup. Empty a packet of Kool-Aid into a cup and add a Tbsp. of water. Stir. Repeat for all the flavors.

Opening Prayer

Song: The World Is So Big   pg. 235 Children's Songbook

Activity: Briefly review the story of Noah (Genesis 6 – 9). Long ago the people on the earth were terribly wicked. Heavenly Father decided to send a flood to wipe the earth clean.

Noah was a righteous man. He was commanded to build a huge ship known as an ark. Two of every kind of animal was in the ark when the rains came. It rained for forty days and forty nights. There was so much water that everything that breathed air died (7:19-22).

But, Noah, his family, and the animals were safe inside the ark. After a long time, the water dried up. The people and animals were able to leave the ark. Noah built an alter and offered sacrifices (8:19-20) to thank the Lord.

Heavenly Father promised to never flood the earth again (9:9-15). The rainbow is a reminder of this promise. Read aloud vs. 14 & 15. When you see a rainbow remember the Lord's promise to never flood the world again.

Everyone take a piece of paper & a few Q-tips. Dip the Q-tips in the Kool-Aid and paint a beautiful scratch-n-sniff rainbow.

Closing Prayer   Quickly read the lesson for next week.

Samuel the Lamanite

Purpose: To increase trust that Heavenly Father will protect us.

Supplies: Materials for simple costume (towels, sheets, bathrobes, etc.)
Pillows, sponges, crumpled newspaper, etc.
Scriptures

Opening Prayer

Song: Follow the Prophet   vs. 6   pg. 110 Children's Songbook

Activity: (Scripture reference: Helamen 13-16) Over time, the Nephites became wicked while the Lamanites become a more righteous people. A Lamanite prophet named Samuel tried to tell the Nephites who lived in a city named Zarahemla to repent. They were angry and threw him out of their city. The Lord instructed his servant Samuel to return and prophesy again. He was to tell them whatever came into his heart. When he returned, Samuel stood on top of the great wall that surrounded the city. (Show the picture of the Prophet Samuel on the Wall, if available.) He warned the people and called them to repentance. He also prophesied many wonderful things about the Savior, saying that he would be born in five years. Samuel told them of wondrous signs that would accompany the birth of the Savior. He also prophesied of Christ's death, and he told them that Jesus would be resurrected and live again. Samuel prophesied of signs that would help the people know these things had indeed happened. The people of Zarahemla were so angry with Samuel that they began to throw stones, and some people tried to shoot him using bows and arrows. Samuel was doing what the Lord had instructed him to do. The Lord protected him. The angry people could not hit him with their stones, nor with their arrows. They tried to capture Samuel, but he jumped down from the wall and quickly returned to his own land where he was safe. Samuel obeyed the Lord, and the Lord protected him.

Dramatize. Stand on a chair, sofa, or bed. Pretend to be Samuel. Use simple costumes. Call the people to repentance. Tell of Christ's birth or death, and of his resurrection. Those playing the part of the angry crowds could use pillows, sponges, or crumpled newspaper to be stones and arrows. Remember not to actually hit Samuel! Samuel jumps down and runs away to avoid the crowds who want to capture him.

Heavenly Father will protect us just as he did Samuel if we are faithful and obedient.

Closing Prayer

Quickly read the lesson for next week.

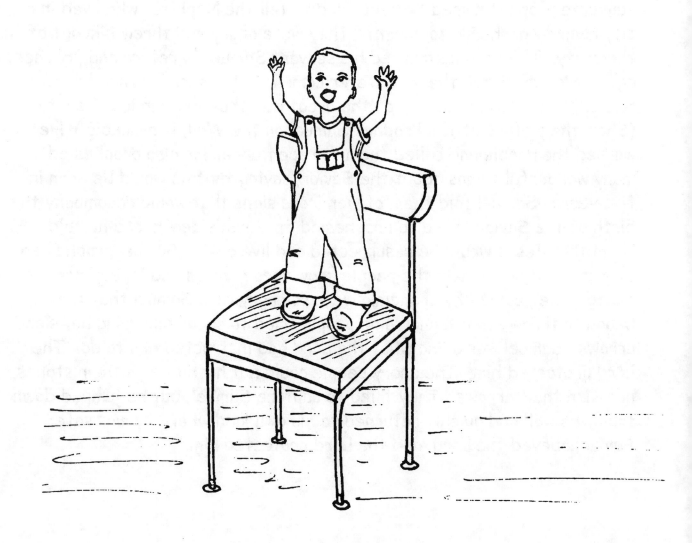

Obedience

Purpose: Increase our desire to be obedient.

Supplies: Apple wedges and nuts   Blankets, bathrobes, towels, etc.
            Scriptures

Opening Prayer

Song: Keep the Commandments   pg. 146 Children's Songbook

Activity: (Scriptural reference: 1 Nephi 2:1-20) The Lord commanded Lehi to leave Jerusalem because the city was going to be destroyed. Lehi was to take his family and go into the wilderness. They would be safe there. It was not an easy thing to do, but Lehi was obedient. He took his wife, Sariah, and their four sons: Laman, Lemuel, Sam, and Nephi. They took tents and provisions, but left their home, wealth, and possessions. They also left all their friends behind. Laman and Lemuel did not want to go. They were angry with their father and they began to murmur. They did not believe Jerusalem would be destroyed. Unlike Laman and Lemuel, Nephi prayed for understanding; the Lord revealed to Nephi the things Lehi had both seen and heard. Nephi shared his knowledge with Sam, then Sam also believed. Laman and Lemuel continued to be rebellious and eventually became disobedient. Nephi was told by the Lord that if he remained obedient, he would be led to a Promised Land, a land which was choice above all others. Nephi trusted the Lord and kept the commandments. He was obedient, and he was blessed.

Throughout the scriptures, those who have been obedient have been blessed. Heavenly Father loves us. He will bless us when we are obedient.

Challenge: Choose an area in which to be more obedient. Examples: daily prayer, scripture study, tithing, less murmuring, etc.

Use simple costumes made from things you have on hand such as blankets, bath robes, towels, anything. Act out the story. While acting out the story, enjoy the apples and nuts. This is one of the things Lehi and his family ate while on their journey through the wilderness.

Closing Prayer   Quickly read the lesson for next week.

Sense of Sight

Purpose: To appreciate the sense of sight.

Note: This lesson could be easily taught by older children to younger siblings.

Supplies: Blindfolds   Scriptures

Opening Prayer

Song: Two Little Eyes   pg. 268   Children's Songbook

Activity: We have mentioned in other lessons that Heavenly Father has created the wonderful world in which we live. What are the five senses that Heavenly Father gave us that enable us to explore and enjoy this world? (sight, hearing, taste, smell, and touch) Read Matthew 13:16. In this lesson we are going to focus on the sense of sight.

What a fantastic blessing sight is. We can see the loving faces of our family, the beautiful colors of a rainbow or sunset, and so much more. Have each member of the family say his/her favorite color. We use our vision (vision means seeing) every day all day long in work and in play. We rely on our sight so much that even seemingly simple tasks would be very difficult without it.

We are going to play a little game that will demonstrate the importance of our sight. Blindfold one member of the family. Now have him/her do a job that is usually quite easy to complete. For example: doing dishes, changing clothes, dusting, dumping the garbage, sweeping, etc. Doing these jobs in the dark is not easy at all. Give each family member the opportunity to be blindfolded and perform a task.

We rely upon our sight so much. We must always be thankful to Heavenly Father for giving us the ability to see and for giving us so many beautiful colors and wonderful sights.

Closing Prayer   Quickly read the lesson for next week.

Manners

Purpose: Help children become more aware of polite behavior.

Supplies: Scriptures

Opening Prayer

Song: Jesus Wants Me for a Sunbeam   pg. 60 Children's Songbook

Activity: (Scriptural reference: John 13:15, 34) To be courteous means to be considerate, respectful, and well mannered. I can learn to be courteous by being kind and polite. I can say "please" and "thank you" and "excuse me." I can share and wait my turn. I can let others finish speaking before I talk. I can cheerfully do as I am asked to do. I can smile. I can speak using a nice tone of voice and polite words. I can be obedient to my parents.

Practice each skill mentioned in the lesson by role-playing. Tell when each polite phrase would be used.

Our manners will improve as we practice polite behavior in our daily lives. It is pleasant to be around people who use good manners.

Closing Prayer

Quickly read the lesson for next week.

Spring

Purpose: To increase appreciation for and awareness of this beautiful season.

Note: The concept of this lesson is easy to understand. It would be a good lesson for older children to teach to younger siblings.

Supplies: Popcorn (optional)   Scriptures

Opening Prayer

Song: Popcorn Popping   pg 242 Children's Songbook

Activity: (Scriptural reference: Song of Solomon 2:11-12) Define spring as a season of the year when seeds begin to sprout and grow. It is a time of "awakening" for the earth. It comes after winter, a time of "sleeping" for the earth. Spring brings forth many beautiful things and is like a new beginning.

Take a little nature walk and snack on the popcorn. Look at the blossoms, flowers, grass, trees leafing out, etc. Look for butterflies, ladybugs, caterpillars, etc. Listen to birds, crickets, etc. Feel the breeze, rain, warmth of the sun, etc.

Challenge: Allow each person time to discuss his/her favorite part of the nature walk.

Reinforce that Heavenly Father has given us each and everyone of these things. We are especially grateful for the spring and all of these wonderful experiences.

Closing Prayer

Quickly read the lesson for next week.

Modern Day Prophets

Purpose: Familiarization with the modern day prophets and their key teachings.

Supplies: Pictures of the prophets (optional)
            Rolled up pair of socks   Scriptures

Opening Prayer

Song: Latter-day Prophets   pg. 134   Children's Songbook

Activity: Heavenly Father has called a person to lead and guide the Church and all its members. This person is called a prophet. Heavenly Father tells the prophet what he wants us to know and do so that we may return to him. Read D & C 1:37-38. Since the Church has been restored there have been many prophets and each one has had a special message for us from the Lord.

1. Joseph Smith   Love one another - even our enemies.
2. Brigham Young   Truth is obeyed when it is loved.
3. John Taylor   God loves all men, everywhere.
4. Wilford Woodruff   Rely on the Holy Ghost.
5. Lorenzo Snow   Pay your tithing and you will be blessed.
6. Joseph F. Smith   Importance of having Family Home Evening.
7. Heber J. Grant   Importance of work
8. George Albert Smith   Stay on the Lord's side.
9. David O. McKay   Every member a missionary.
10. Joseph Fielding Smith   The Gospel is for everyone in the entire world.
11. Harold B. Lee   Importance of keeping the commandments.
12. Spencer W. Kimball   Lengthen your stride.
13. Ezra Taft Benson   Read and study the Book of Mormon
14. Howard W. Hunter   Be worthy to go to the temple.
15. Gordon B. Hinckley   Love those that are different.

Review this list with your family. Make sure the children understand what each prophet is trying to teach us. For example: Spencer W. Kimball told us to lengthen our stride. That means to work hard and do all that you can for each and every task whether it be for school, home, or church.

Now grab the sock ball and play a game to help remember the prophets and the teachings they have given us. Get everyone in a circle. Toss the ball from person to person in order or randomly. One person will say a prophet and the next will say that prophet's special teaching. Another variation is to pass the ball around trying to list the prophets in order. Once you have mastered forward, try listing the prophets in reverse order. Refer to the list often to help you play the games. However, you will be surprised how quickly you learn the prophets and their teachings.

All of these men are very special and have been called of Heavenly Father to lead us. If we will follow their teachings and examples we will be able to live with Heavenly Father again.

Closing Prayer

Quickly review the lesson for next week.

Rocky Road

Purpose: To give our burdens unto the Lord.

Supplies: Rocky Road ice cream or Rocky Road candy bars
             Scriptures

Opening Prayer

Song: Be Happy!   pg. 265 Children's Songbook

Activity: Our lives are very busy. Whether we are big or small, we have many responsibilities. Give everyone in the family the opportunity to name some of his/her jobs. For example: work, meal preparation, church callings, school, homework, various chores such as keeping your room clean, dumping the garbage, walking the dog, etc.

Sometimes it feels like our burdens are too heavy. We must always remember that we will not be given more than we can handle. The Lord knows us better than we know ourselves, and he knows what we can do.

We must also remember that we are not alone with our burdens on this rocky road called life. Read Psalms 55:22. The Lord will help us with our burdens if we but ask in faith.

One of the ways Heavenly Father eases our burdens, tasks, and responsibilities is by giving us a family. We are here to help love and support each other. By helping each other, we can make each other's burdens lighter and the road less rocky. What are some ways we can help each other? Examples are: helping with preparing the meals, picking up our toys, doing our homework without being told, etc.

Challenge: Trust the Lord. Give him your burdens and you will be happier.

Enjoy the Rocky Road ice cream or candy bars and discuss ways we can help each other.

Closing Prayer   Quickly read the lesson for next week.

Gardens

Purpose: Give children an opportunity to plant seeds and watch them grow and mature.

Supplies: Seeds   Potting soil
             Pot or paper cup   Water
             Scriptures

Opening Prayer

Song: The Prophet Said to Plant a Garden   pg. 237 Children's Songbook

Activity: Using pots or other containers, use potting soil, seeds, and water to start a garden. This may be adapted to plant seeds or transplant started plants to a garden bed.

It takes faith to believe that tiny seeds buried in the soil will become large plants that will give fruit, vegetables or flowers in return for the care they are given.

The prophet has told us to plant a garden. We can show our obedience by our actions tonight. Not only are we demonstrating obedience but we are also learning self-reliance. This is another thing that the prophets have asked us to do. Read D & C 64:34.

By using food from the garden, money is saved. It can be used to help the family or donated to needy people.

As we demonstrate obedience by planting a garden, our efforts will be rewarded as the seeds grow and mature. I am thankful for the fruit, vegetables, and flowers that grow from these tiny seeds.

Closing Prayer

Quickly read the lesson for next week.

Make Our Homes a Safer Place

Purpose: Help each family member realize his/her part in creating a cleaner and safer environment.

Supplies: None

Opening Prayer

Song: A Happy Family   pg. 198 Children's Songbook

Activity: Why is a safe home something to be desired? We love our family members. ". . .the beloved of the Lord shall dwell in safety. . ." (Deuteronemy 33:12) We want them to be well and safe from accidents that could cause them to be hurt. We can help create a home that is safer. By cleaning up, picking up, and being aware of problem areas, we can help to make our home a safer place. We can work together to do this.

Go from room to room. Discuss what could be done to create a safer environment. Note safety hazards and possible solutions to problems.

Kitchen: Don't touch the stove because it could be hot and burn you. Don't play with knives. They are sharp and can cut. Get an adult when you need to use a knife. If a glass breaks, get an adult to sweep up the sharp pieces of glass. Add safety tips that suit your own family's needs.

Bathroom: Don't use electrical appliances near water. They can cause an electrical shock that may be deadly. Pick up clothes and towels after bathing. Wipe up wet spots on the floor to prevent slipping. Stay seated in the tub to reduce the risk of falling. Add your own tips.

Stairs: Pick up toys and clutter to reduce the risk of falling.

Bedrooms: Pick up toys and clothes to ensure a clear pathway. Clutter makes it easier to trip and fall. Keep little objects out of the reach of children under three (3) years of age to reduce the risk of choking. Do not put anything in electrical outlets. Add your own tips.

Garage/cleaning closet: Use "Mr. Yuck" stickers on poisonous materials and discuss with children not to touch, smell, or drink these substances because of the potentially fatal results. Hazardous substances should be put out of the reach of children, and locked up if possible. Add your own tips as suits your family's needs.

Reduce clutter in all rooms since clutter is fuel for fire. Newspapers, rags, etc. should have a place designated where they can be stored until they are needed. If they will not be needed, they should be disposed of.

Accidents happen regardless of the effort one takes, but a safer environment can help reduce the risk of injury related to falls, burns, cuts, choking, etc. It's everybody's job to help make the home a safe place. Because we love each other, we want to do all we can to help.

Challenge: Memorize 911. Place the phone number for the Poison Control Center (1-800-860-0620) near each phone.

Closing Prayer

As the children grow older and are better able to understand more complex issues, discuss safety from a different angle. For instance, telephone safety, 911 emergency calls, locking doors and windows, not opening the door to strangers, proper lighting, etc. Again, add safety rules that best fit your family's needs.

Quickly read the lesson for next week.

Family Ten Commandments

Purpose: To review the story of Moses and the Ten Commandments.

Supplies: Scriptures   Pencils/Pens   Paper
            Picture of Moses with the Ten Commandments (optional)

Opening Prayer

Song: Keep the Commandments   pg. 146 Children's Songbook

Activity: Very long ago, there was a group of people known as the Israelites. They were slaves to Pharaoh, the Egyptian king. The Pharaoh treated them badly and they wanted to be free. Heavenly Father heard their pleas and sent a man named Moses to lead them out of bondage.

It was not an easy task but Moses was able to take the Israelites out of Egypt. For forty years, the Israelites wandered the dessert until they were righteous enough to enter the Promised Land. While traveling, Heavenly Father gave Moses rules for the Israelites to live by. These rules were known as the Ten Commandments. If available, show the picture of Moses.

Read Exodus 20:3-4, 7-8, 12-17. Explain that taking the Lord's name in vain (vs. 7) means swearing or saying bad words. "Honor thy father and mother" (vs. 12) means to obey them. "Bear false witness" (vs. 16) means to lie or gossip. "Covet" (vs. 17) means to strongly desire something that belongs to someone else.

These rules were given long ago but they are just as important today. We must obey them if we are to be worthy to return to our Father in Heaven.

Having a few more rules won't hurt. Give each family member a pencil and piece of paper. Have everyone create his/her own Ten Commandments. Possible commandments are to knock before entering a bedroom, put all dirty laundry in the hamper, etc. Or do the activity as a family where everyone inputs to create Family Ten Commandments. A common yet excellent rule is No Whining! Enjoy.

Closing Prayer   Quickly read the lesson for next week

Listen to the Holy Ghost

Purpose: Heavenly Father has given us the Holy Ghost to guide us and help us make right choices.

Supplies: Scriptures
Plate of goodies, a sweet treat of some kind, bowl of apples, pretzels, anything

Advance preparation: Before everyone is called together to begin Family Home Evening, hide the plate of goodies someplace difficult.

Opening Prayer

Song: The Still Small Voice   pg. 106 Children's Songbook

Activity: Read aloud D&C 11:12 & 13. Heavenly Father has given us the gift of the Holy Ghost. The Holy Ghost will lead us, guide us, comfort us, and enlighten us throughout our entire lives if we remain worthy. However, the Holy Ghost does not shout. He speaks with a still small voice. It is quiet like a whisper. We must follow the commandments of the Lord so that we will be able to hear these whispers. Have each family member name something that we can do to help us be able to hear the soft voice of the Holy Ghost. For example: reading the scriptures, praying and then listening, attending our church meetings, etc.

Tell the children what you have hidden but don't tell them where. Have the person who hid the item softly whisper hints as to its location, and also explain that the person whispering represents the Holy Ghost. The children will need to listen closely to find it.

If we listen carefully, the Holy Ghost will guide us to life with Heavenly Father. Our challenge will be to learn to recognize and to listen to the promptings of the Holy Ghost.

Closing Prayer

Quickly read the lesson for next week.

The Cornerstone

Purpose: To teach children that Jesus Christ is the cornerstone of the church.

Supplies: Bag of big marshmallows or box of sugar cubes
Scriptures

Opening Prayer

Song: The Church of Jesus Christ   pg. 77 Children's Songbook

Activity: Begin by explaining that a cornerstone is a stone that is placed first and the remaining building is built on and around it. If this cornerstone were to be removed the entire building would fall down.

Jesus Christ is the cornerstone of our church. This means that the entire church is built upon his examples, actions, and teachings. Read Ephesians 5:1. The Church of Jesus Christ of Latter-day Saints will never crumble because Jesus, as the cornerstone, will always be there to love and guide us back to eternal life with Heavenly Father.

Get the marshmallows or sugar cubes. Designate a specific marshmallow or sugar cube to be the cornerstone. Use your imagination and build a building. Demonstrate how the entire structure collapses when the cornerstone is removed. Again emphasize that our church is built upon Jesus' example and teachings. They will never be changed nor will they be taken from the earth.

Closing Prayer

Quickly read the lesson for next week.

King Benjamin's Tower

Purpose: Learn to listen to and heed the words of our leaders.

Supplies: Chair   Scriptures

Opening Prayer

Song: Teach me to Walk in the Light   pg. 177 Children's Songbook

Object: King Benjamin was a good man. He loved his people very much and wanted to share many things with them before he died. He ordered that all the people of the kingdom come to the temple to hear his words. So many people came that King Benjamin had a tower built (Mosiah 2:7-8) so everyone could hear him.

King Benjamin told the people to always help one another. When you help people, you are helping Heavenly Father (vs. 17 – 18). We should be thankful to Heavenly Father for all the blessings he has given us (vs. 20). Also, we need to obey his commandments for if we do, Heavenly Father will bless and preserve us (vs. 22).

King Benjamin also foretold of the coming of Christ and of the miracles he would perform (Mosiah 3:5). He also told of the pain Jesus would suffer for us (vs. 7), the sacrifice he would make for us (vs. 9), and of his resurrection from the dead (vs. 10).

King Benjamin said many more important things. When he was through, the people wanted to repent and to be good. Heavenly Father forgave them. King Benjamin was very happy to be able to talk to his people. He was also happy for their choice to repent and be a righteous people.

Now each family member can give words of advice just as King Benjamin did. Take turns standing upon a chair and share any lesson, advice, or truth you have learned. For example: don't run across the playground with your shoes untied. This is a very important safety tip. Share anything.

Closing Prayer   Quickly read the lesson for next week.

Tithing

Purpose: To demonstrate that tithing is 10% and to discuss the many ways tithing is used.

Supplies: Pretzels   M&Ms   Peanuts
            Raisins   Anything else you like in trail mix
            Two bowls   Scriptures

Opening Prayer

Song: I'm Glad to Pay a Tithing   pg. 150 Children's Songbook

Activity: We have been asked by the Prophet to pay tithing. Read D & C 119:4. For whatever we have (in pioneer time it was harvested crops but today it is usually money), we have been commanded to give one-tenth to the church. To demonstrate: take two bowls. One is for the family and the other is for the church. Take the pretzels and have the children count out ten. Then have them put one in the bowl for the church and the remaining nine in the bowl for the family. Do this several more times with the pretzels then continue with the M&Ms, peanuts, raisins, etc. until you have a nice sized bowl of trail mix. (The children will get very good at counting to ten.) Put the two bowls side by side. See how large the bowl for the family is compared to the bowl for the church. The Lord asks us to sacrifice and give one-tenth but there will always be enough for the family. This is one of the blessings of tithing. If we pay our tithing we will have enough for our needs.

Now refer to the bowl of trail mix which represents tithing. What is tithing used for? It is used to build temples, maintain church houses, provide food and other necessary items to families in need, and print Books of Mormon & lesson manuals. A portion of our tithing goes to ward budgets which allows for activities that strengthen friendships and increase fellowshipping. These are just a few uses of tithing. Give every family member the opportunity to think of more.

One of the uses of tithing previously mentioned was for strengthening friendships and fellowshipping. We can do that this evening. Take the bowl of trail mix designated as tithing to a friend or a neighbor. Give it to them along with a smile. Perhaps you could take the larger bowl of trail mix, visit awhile, and enjoy the evening.

Challenge: Designate a chore for each child for which money will be earned. Help the children calculate what an honest tithe would be for the money they earn. Also, using a tithing slip, discuss each section as the children fill it out.

Never hesitate to pay an honest tithing. The Lord will bless you for your faithfulness and your needs will be met.

Closing Prayer

Quickly read the lesson for next week.

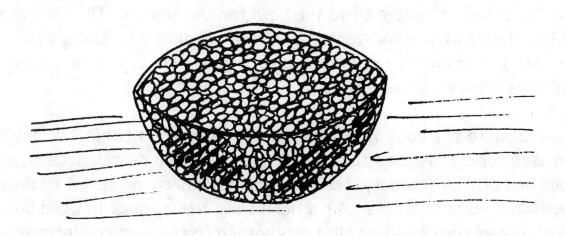

Playdoh World

Purpose: To explain that we if we are faithful and obedient we may become like Heavenly Father.

Supplies: Scriptures   Playdoh

Opening Prayer

Song: All Things Bright and Beautiful   pg. 231 Children's Songbook

Activity: What are we? Read Psalms 82:6. We are children of Heavenly Father. We have the potential to become gods and goddesses like him. If we have faith, obey the commandments, follow the prophet, etc., we can become like Heavenly Father.

Heavenly Father has a tremendous amount of power. Read Mosiah 4:9. Heavenly Father has created all things in heaven and on earth including us. To be like him and to have power such as his is our potential. Have every family member say something that we must do to be worthy to return to Heavenly Father and be like him. Examples are: read, study and ponder the scriptures, love one another, pray constantly, attend church meetings, etc.

If we are righteous, we will be able to become like Heavenly Father. If we achieve our full potential, we will have the opportunity to create our own worlds. We can practice now using the Playdoh to sculpt animals and plants.

Closing Prayer

Quickly read the lesson for next week.

Self Esteem

Purpose: Help each child learn to feel good about him or herself.

Supplies: Scriptures

Opening Prayer

Song: I Am a Child of God   pg. 2 Children's Songbook

Activity: I am a spirit child of Heavenly Father. Jesus Christ is my brother. I am special. Heavenly Father has blessed me with a family, a home, a beautiful world in which to live, etc. I have special talents. I am unique. No one else is exactly like me. Have each member of the family say something that makes him/her unique or different from everybody else.

Each one of us has wonderful qualities such as a happy attitude, a giving/ sharing nature, an acceptance of others, etc. Often it is hard to see these qualities in ourselves but other people can see them. Have each family member point out a nice quality for every person in the family. It is really great to hear these things about ourselves. Remember these things and feel good about the unique person you are.

Have an impromptu talent show to celebrate our individual talents. Possible talents for the younger children are: hop on one leg, skip, walk backward, sing, whisper, wink, clap hands, clap hands behind back, make a funny face, etc.

There is nobody else exactly like me. My family loves me. Heavenly Father and Jesus Christ love me and I am special. Read D & C 18:10.

Closing Prayer

Quickly read the lesson for next week.

Sense of Hearing and Smell

Purpose: To be more aware of and appreciate the senses of hearing and smell.

Supplies: Small amount of money (optional)
            Home baked rolls or cookies (optional)

Opening Prayer

Song: I Have Two Ears   pg. 269 Children's Songbook

Activity: Heavenly Father has created a fantastic world for us to live in. Quite often we do not stop to appreciate the things around us, recognize Heavenly Father's hand, and thank him. Today we are going to talk about the senses of hearing and smell. We enjoy so many things in the world because of these senses.

Hearing. "But blessed are your . . . ears, for they hear." (Matthew 13:16) We can hear everything from the soft sound of a kitten purring to the enormous roar of a crowd when a touchdown is scored. Have each family member say his/her favorite sound. Through hearing, we can enjoy our family's happy laughs, silly whispered jokes, and shouts of joy when we succeed. How blessed we are.

Smell. What a miracle it is to be able to smell. Our nose can ferret out all sorts of unique smells from gym socks that should have been washed months ago to Grandma's mouth watering homemade bread. Have each family member say his/her favorite smell. How blessed we are.

We are now going to put these senses to the test and demonstrate how much hearing and smelling tell us about our world. As a family, go for a little walk. Mosey around for a little while. Perhaps allow each family member to have a turn at being leader. While you are walking, play a game with hearing and smelling. It is similar to eye-spy except say "with my little ear, I hear. . .something with wings" and then everyone tries to guess what you are hearing. It could be a bird, mosquito, plane, etc. Also say "with my little nose, it goes. . .something sweet" and then everyone tries to guess what you are smelling. It could be perfume, sweet rolls from a bakery, flowers, etc.

Optional addition: during your walking and playing you may pass a hot dog vendor or pretzel stand. If you have a little money you could also enjoy the sense of taste. Or bring homemade bread/rolls or cookies (They smell so good!) to enjoy.

Heavenly Father has blessed us tremendously. We are able to enjoy and explore this world through our senses. We must always remember to stop and appreciate the things Heavenly Father has given us and say thank you for everything.

Closing Prayer

Quickly read the lesson for next week.

Pioneers

Purpose: Help children be more aware of the pioneers' tasks, work, and lives.

Supplies: Bicycle, tricycle, wagon, or anything with a wheel (Small toys such as hot wheel cars will not work for this activity.)
Scarf or handkerchief
Scriptures

Opening Prayer

Song: Little Pioneer Children   pg. 216 Children's Songbook

Activity: If possible, sit outside in a circle. Today we are going to talk about pioneers. Pioneers are people who sacrificed much to follow the prophet and helped to build God's kingdom in the west. Discuss differences between their times and our times regarding transportation, clothing styles, chips (usually buffalo manure) for firewood, cooking over an open fire, the lack of luxuries, little food and water, illness, etc. Tell of children's duties which included feeding and watering the animals, gathering firewood or chips, helping in the garden, tending younger family members, making butter, etc. Act out some of these chores as they are discussed. Another task given to children in wagon trains was to keep track of the distance traveled each day. The children did this by tying a scarf or handkerchief to a spoke on the wagon wheel and counting how many times it went around. This would be a very dizzying task. Give it a try yourselves by tying a scarf or handkerchief to a spoke on a bicycle, tricycle, or wagon. Go for a ride and have the children walk along side and count the rotations of the scarf. Easier said than done.

The pioneers had a hard life but they also valued wholesome entertainment. They had music and dances. Read D & C 136:28. They created fun out of work by holding sewing bees, quilting parties, and log sawing contests. They helped each other clear land of trees and dig trenches and canals to drain swampy ground. They worked together to build log houses and barns. They sacrificed much but the Lord blessed their efforts.

We need to be as steadfast in following our prophet today as the pioneers were in their day. We can follow the pioneer's example by doing as our prophet asks. For instance, we can read the Book of Mormon, have Family Home Evening, family prayer, etc.

Challenge: Learn the words and music to a pioneer song, or try not to use any electricity for a one to two hour block of time.

Closing Prayer

Quickly read the lesson for next week.

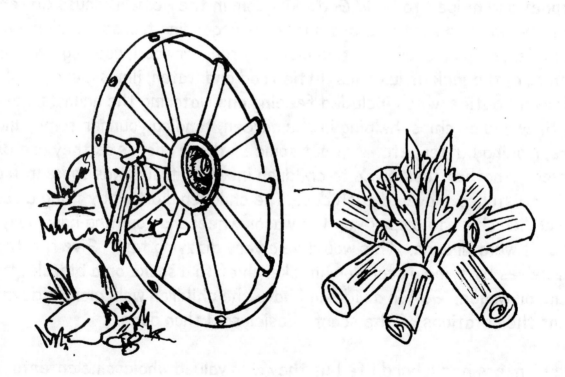

Play It Again, Sam

Purpose: Repeat one of the lessons to emphasize the message.

Supplies: Depends upon which lesson you wish to repeat

Opening Prayer

Song: Hinges   pg. 277 Children's Songbook

Activity: We learn through repetition. Here is the opportunity to go back and repeat your family's favorite lesson. Play, learn, enjoy and remember.

Closing Prayer

Quickly read the lesson for next week.

The Burning Bush

Purpose: Emphasize reverence.

Supplies: Sticks (about two feet long) or kabob skewers
Candles   Matches
Large marshmallows   Scriptures

Opening Prayer

Song: Reverently, Quietly   pg. 26 Children's Songbook

Activity: We are going to talk about Moses today. Who was Moses? He was a righteous man that lived long ago. He freed the Israelites from bondage and received the Ten Commandments. Turn to Exodus 3:2-4. These verses talk about the first time Heavenly Father spoke to Moses. Read these verses aloud and explain that "the bush burned with fire, and the bush was not consumed" (vs. 2) means that the bush was burning but was not turned to ashes.

Read verse 5 aloud. Moses was commanded to remove his shoes for he stood upon holy ground. Today we do not remove our shoes but we are commanded to be reverent in holy places. Holy places include the entire church building but especially the Chapel. We should not run or yell but instead we should walk reverently, quietly, and with folded arms.

We should also be reverent in our Primary and Sunday School classes. The Lord spoke to Moses through a burning bush. The Lord speaks to us through our parents, church leaders, teachers, and the Holy Ghost. We should be quietly listening and learning.

Here's the fun. Under close adult supervision, light the candles and roast the marshmallows. Wouldn't it be wonderful if Heavenly Father would talk to us out of the flame of our candles like he spoke to Moses from the burning bush? Perhaps he would say that he loves us and is proud of the hard work we are doing? Perhaps he would encourage us to choose the right and pray often? Discuss what Heavenly Father might say to us while enjoying the marshmallows.

Closing Prayer   Quickly read the lesson for next week.

Our Bodies are a Wonderful Gift

Purpose: To help increase appreciation for our bodies and recognize them as a gift from Heavenly Father.

Supplies: Scriptures   Scarf or length of cloth for blindfold

Opening Prayer

Song: Head, Shoulders, Knees, and Toes   pg. 275 Children's Songbook

Activity: Read aloud Genesis 1:27. Name the parts of your face (eyes nose, mouth, ears). Which of these do we use to hear? To smell? To speak? And to eat? Close your eyes. What can you see? Open your eyes. Now what can you see? Cover your ears. What can you hear? Uncover your ears. Now what can you hear? Name parts of the body (arms, hands, legs, feet). Experiment with the following, if we didn't have arms, could we hug anybody? Could we hold anything? If we didn't have our hands, could we wave goodbye? Pet an animal? Comb our hair? If we didn't have our legs and feet, could we run, hop, skip, or jump? Without a nose we would miss the smell of baking bread and cookies, and we couldn't smell the scent of a flower or smell the earth after a rain. Without mouths, we couldn't eat, talk, sing, or say "I love you."

Blindfold a volunteer, then ask him/her to do something that requires eyesight such as read a book, newspaper, etc. Use the soft cloth to tie legs together, then ask the volunteer to dance, etc. Ask a volunteer to clasp his/her hands behind his/her back. Then ask the volunteer to open a door, shake hands, etc. Take turns doing these activities. Highlight how wonderful our bodies are and how grateful we are for them.

Challenge: For a week concentrate on one body part (eyes, hands, legs, etc.) paying particular attention to how much it is used every day.

Because our bodies are such a wonderful gift, let's use them by closing our eyes, bowing our heads, folding our arms, and quietly using our voices to pray our thanks to Heavenly Father.

Closing Prayer

Quickly read the lesson for next week.

Optional discussion topics for families with older children: Word of Wisdom, modesty, or exercise and good health practices such as good nutrition, regular dental and medical check-ups.

Feast Upon the Word

Purpose: Enjoy the words of Christ and apply them to our lives.

Supplies: Fast food or dinner that is a family favorite
Scriptures

Opening Prayer

Song: I'm Trying to Be like Jesus   pg. 78 Children's Songbook

Activity: Everyone gather around the table with napkins, drinks, forks, etc. Food should be ready to eat. Turn to 2 Nephi 32:3 and read it aloud. We have been commanded to feast upon the words of the Lord. That does not mean to take a little nibble but to really eat heartily. We should apply the words of Christ to our lives and try to follow his example in all that we do.

Enjoy your dinner. While you are eating, take turns sharing favorite scriptures, quotes from the prophets, Primary songs, scriptures and church history stories. Feast upon your favorite words of the Lord as you feast upon your favorite dinner.

Closing Prayer

Quickly read the lesson for next week.

Title of Liberty

Purpose: To develop a sense of patriotism.

Supplies: An old shirt or a piece of cloth   Markers
          Yardstick or broom handle or baton, etc.   Scriptures

Opening Prayer

Song: My Country 'Tis of Thee

Activity: (Scripture reference: Alma 46:12) Moroni was a good man who loved the Lord. He was appointed chief captain over all the Nephite armies. Captain Moroni had sworn an oath to defend his people and their freedom. Another man, Amalickiah, wanted to be king. He was a wicked man. He wanted power over other people. He convinced many people that they would be happier if they were ruled by a king instead of a chief judge. Moroni knew that a king would destroy the freedom the Nephites fought to gain. Moroni also knew that under the influence of an evil king, righteous people could no longer worship God. To rally support, Moroni took off his coat and wrote on it "In memory of our God, our religion, and freedom, and our peace, our wives, and our children." He attached it to a pole and called it the "Title of Liberty." Moroni prayed, then he went among the people waving the banner and asking for supporters for his cause. People gathered. They were ready to fight for their freedom. A renewed love for their country was awakened in the hearts of the people.

Heavenly Father has given us a choice land in which to live. We need to remember the freedom that we enjoy and ask to keep our country free.

On a scrap of material, or an old shirt, write the words as quoted above. Tape it to a broom, yardstick, baton, etc. Parade through the house, yard, or around the block, calling for those who will fight to defend their freedom to join you.

Challenge: Choose one way to practice patriotism. Examples: learn words and music to a patriotic song, review the history of our national flag, or learn the Pledge of Allegiance.

Closing Prayer   Quickly read the lesson for next week.

Emergency Preparedness

Purpose: To prepare an emergency escape route.

Supplies: Paper   Watch with second hand
           Pencils, crayons, markers, stencils, stickers

Opening Prayer

Song: Here We Are Together   pg. 261 Children's Songbook

Activity: It is always a good idea to be prepared for anything that may happen. Can you think of some reasons why we would have to leave our homes quickly? (Keep this light-hearted.)

Prepare an evacuation plan for your family. Evacuation means to leave quickly. Take the piece of paper and draw a sketch of your home. Include all the major rooms and exits in the picture. To involve the children, let them decorate their rooms in the picture with crayons, stickers, stencils, etc.

Once the map is complete, show the children the quickest way out. Discuss escape routes from various rooms in the house, and emphasize the escape routes from their rooms.

Decide on a place outside where the family will gather. Select a safe gathering area, preferably a place that does not require crossing a street.

Practice some of the escape routes and meet at the gathering place. As an added challenge, you might time yourselves to see how long it takes, then try to beat that time at your next attempt.

Heavenly Father has counseled: ". . .if ye are prepared ye shall not fear." (D&C 38:30) Now is the time to prepare.

Challenge: Review and practice the escape routes every three months.

Closing Prayer   Quickly read the lesson for next week.

Sense of Touch

Purpose: To be thankful for the sense of touch.

Note: This lesson could be easily taught by older children to younger siblings.

Supplies: Blindfold

Opening Prayer

Song: I Have Two Little Hands   pg. 272 Children's Songbook

Activity: The world around us is so wonderful. Heavenly Father made everything in it. "And God saw every thing that he had made, and, behold, it was very good." (Genesis 1:31) He then gave us our senses so that we might explore and enjoy all the world has to offer. What are our senses? (Seeing, hearing, smelling, tasting, and touching).

Touch is usually the first sense that we focus on. What is the first thing a baby does with a new object? The baby puts it into his/her mouth which is very sensitive to different textures and temperatures (hot/cold). Texture means how something feels. For example: hard, soft, smooshy, bumpy, prickly, etc.

We learn so much from the shape and texture of things. We are going to play a game that will emphasize just how much we rely on our sense of touch. Take the blindfold and blindfold a member of the family. Give the other members of the family one minute to obtain an object of some sort. When everyone has returned, allow the blindfolded person to feel each object and try to identify it. Allow everyone the opportunity to be blindfolded and identify objects.

The sense of touch is amazing. It tells us so much about where we are and what things are. We must always remember to thank Heavenly Father for this world, for everything in it, and especially for the sense of touch.

Closing Prayer
Quickly read the lesson for next week.

Autumn

Purpose: To increase appreciation for and awareness of the season.
Note: This is an easy lesson for older children to teach.

Supplies: Apple cider or hot cocoa (optional)   Scriptures

Opening Prayer

Song: It's Autumn time   pg. 246 Children's Songbook

Activity: Begin by reading D & C 59:18. Heavenly Father made four seasons which are winter, spring, summer, and fall. Everything in each season was made by Heavenly Father to bring us joy and happiness. Today we are going to experience fall otherwise known as autumn. Autumn is the peaceful time after summer. The crops are ripened and harvested, the food for the winter has been stored by all the busy animals such as squirrels, bees, etc., and the days and nights are becoming cooler in preparation for winter.

Take a walk outside. Notice how the leaves are changing color from green to shades of red, orange and gold. How many different colors and leaf patterns can you find? Notice how you don't find as many insects like ants or bees. They are tucked away for the winter. Name a few ways animals prepare for the winter. Bears and skunks go to sleep, birds fly to warmer climates, and others such as squirrels store food. Notice the grass "going to sleep" in preparation for winter. Enjoy your walk. Enjoy the brisk air. Listen to the peaceful sounds. Delight in the vivid colors all around.

Talk about autumn as a time of preparation, while enjoying the apple cider or cocoa. What can we do to prepare for the winter? Perhaps dig out warm boots & clothes, bring in and clean up toys from outside, or stash away a nice coloring book for the winter months. Give each family member the opportunity to suggest something.

Challenge: Choose one activity to complete during the week that will help prepare for winter.

Closing Prayer   Quickly read the lesson for next week.

Tower of Babel

Purpose: Remind us to be humble.

Supplies: Scriptures   Deck of Old Maid, Go Fish, or any kind of cards

Opening Prayer

Song: Children All Over the World   pg. 16 Children's Songbook

Activity: Open the scriptures to Genesis 11:1-4 and read aloud. Explain to the children, that at this point in time everyone on the earth lived in one place and spoke one language. They had become very prideful and thought they could build a tower all the way to heaven. They wanted to be famous.

Heavenly Father ended work on the tower by confounding the language. Read verses 6-8. Explain that confounding the language means that instead of everyone speaking one language, people suddenly spoke many different languages.

It is hard to get things done when you can't speak to and understand one another. Read verse 9. The people quit working on the tower and scattered across the world. This is why there are so many different languages in the world today.

(Interesting point: The brother of Jared asked Heavenly Father not to confound the language of his family and friends. He didn't change their language and they were known as the Jaredites. Ether 1:33-37)

For fun, try to build a tower using cards. As each card is added to the tower, say a language. For example, add a card and say Swahili, Deutch, Italian, etc. See how tall your tower can get and how many different languages you can name. Also, you can try giving instructions on how to build the card tower in different languages. For example, give directions in French, Spanish, sign language, pig-latin, etc. to demonstrate how confusing instructions in another language are. Perhaps this is what the people at the Tower of Babel actually felt.

Closing Prayer   Quickly read the lesson for next week.

I Can Be Quiet and Respectful in Church

Purpose: Help children learn that they can be quiet, reverent, and respectful in church.

Supplies: Kitchen timer or watch with a second hand
Scriptures

Opening Prayer

Song: The Chapel Doors   pg. 156 Children's Songbook

Activity: Read Leviticus 19:30. "Reverence my sanctuary. . ." means to behave in special places such as church. We are going to practice how to behave in church. Do the following:

Action:	Explanation:
1. Wash face and hands.	I must be clean in the Lord's house.
2. Comb hair.	I must be well-groomed in the Lord's house.
3. Think of quiet, peaceful things, or sing a Primary song quietly to yourself.	I can fill my mind with thoughts of Heavenly Father and Jesus Christ.
4. Keep legs/feet still. See which family member can be still the longest. (Use the timer.)	I can learn to control my movements.
5. Keep arms/hands still. See which family member can be still the longest. (Use the timer.)	I can learn to keep my hands to myself.
6. Do not talk for two minutes. See which family member can be quiet the longest. (Use the timer.)	I can choose when to speak.
7. Whisper, then talk in a regular voice, then use a loud "outside" voice.	I can control how loud I speak.

46

It may be hard to sit still and to be quiet for long periods of time. It's hard to learn control. Hard things require practice. It will become easier as one grows older and gains experience. Heavenly Father and Jesus Christ are pleased when people are able to sit quietly. They are also pleased when people fill their minds with good thoughts, scripture stories, or good music. With practice we can learn to act reverently and respectfully in church.

Closing Prayer

Remember to praise the children's efforts and acknowledge when progress is made. Give this lesson again in three or four months as a progress check.

Quickly read the lesson for next week.

Line Upon Line

Purpose: To teach the importance of learning lessons well.

Supplies: Bread   Peanut butter   Jelly
               Butter knife   Scriptures

Opening Prayer

Song: Teach Me to Walk in the Light   pg. 177 Children's Songbook

Activity: Begin the activity by having the children instruct the adults how to make a peanut butter and jelly sandwich. (The key to this activity is to do exactly what the children say. For example: If they say to put the peanut butter on the bread. Pick up the jar of peanut butter and place it on the bread sack. This activity can be very fun.) Making a peanut butter and jelly sandwich seems like a very simple job but it actually takes numerous steps to do.

Life is full of activities that may seem easy but actually require the mastery of many smaller tasks. One cannot pick up a pencil and write sentences from the very beginning. One must learn the alphabet, practice drawing lines and circles, learn each individual letter and how to put them together to make words, and finally put words together to make sentences. Can you think of other examples?

The gospel of Jesus Christ is the same way. We are not expected to know everything from the very beginning. We learn things a little at a time. The lessons we learn build upon each other. Read 2 Nephi 28:30. Name something that we have learned a little at a time, practiced, and now can do very well. For example: Prayer. First, parents say a prayer and then the children repeat it. Next, children are able to say the prayer, but it is always the same without variation. Eventually, children are able to say a prayer that contains variety and depth of feeling.

48

Heavenly Father gives us information line upon line. We gain this information from many sources. Can you think of and name different places, people, or things from which we learn? (Primary and Sunday School teachers, Sacrament meeting, the scriptures, Mom & Dad, etc.)

There is a great deal to learn about the gospel of Jesus Christ. We need to learn our lessons very well. Our knowledge will increase day by day as we learn line by line.

Challenge: Learn something new about the gospel through a teacher or the scriptures. Share your new knowledge with a parent, brother, or sister.

Enjoy the peanut butter and jelly sandwiches.

Closing Prayer

Quickly read the lesson for next week.

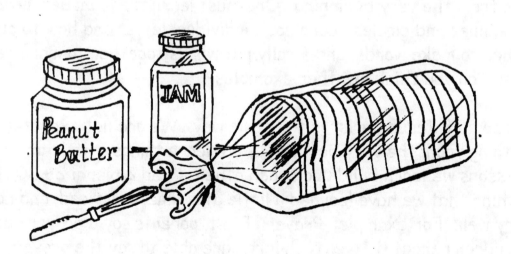

God's Image

Purpose: To teach that we are created in Heavenly Father's image and are all equal in his sight.

Supplies: Scriptures
            Music to the Hokey Pokey (not required)

Opening Prayer

Song: I Have Two Ears   pg. 269 Children's Songbook

Activity: Turn to and read aloud Genesis 1:26-27. This means that Heavenly Father made us just like he is made. He has two ears. We have two ears. He has two arms and legs. We have two arms and legs. He has a beautiful smile and loving eyes. We have beautiful smiles and loving eyes. We are made in Heavenly Father's image.

Sometimes we may see people with different skin colors. Some people have black, brown, white or other skin colors. But that does not make them different. All these people still have two ears, two arms & legs, beautiful smiles, and loving eyes. Heavenly Father made us all and loves us all the same.

Everyone sing & dance a few rounds of the Hokey Pokey. Put in those arms, legs, hips and so forth that Heavenly Father created and shake them all about.

Closing Prayer

Quickly read the lesson for next week.

Law of Sacrifice

Purpose: To teach children the meaning of sacrifice.

Supplies: Rock   Scriptures
            Cookies/candy/sweet treat of some kind
            Two sandwich bags

Advance Preparation: In one of the bags place a cookie or two. In the other bag, place three or four cookies and stash it out of sight.

Opening Prayer

Song: "Give," Said the Little Stream   pg. 236 Children's Songbook

Activity: This activity will help explain sacrifice. Give a child the rock and the bag with one or two cookies/candies in it. Ask the child to sacrifice one of them. He/she will probably give up the rock. Explain that giving up the rock is not true sacrifice. One must give up something good to be truly sacrificing. Ask the child to sacrifice again. He/she should give up the cookies. The Lord rewards us when we sacrifice by giving us something better. Using the bag of three or four cookies/candies that you stashed earlier, give it to the child. Sacrifice is hard to do but we will be rewarded with something better as a result.

Throughout the Church's history there have been examples of sacrifice. Often the pioneers gave up their homes, their friends, and sometimes even their families to travel west where they helped to build a temple, a city, and a new life. But what exactly is sacrifice? The definition of sacrifice is the giving up of something good for something better. What would you be willing to sacrifice for your faith? Your home, toys, winter coat, TV/movies, food?

Emphasize that the Lord will always give us something better but it may not be immediate. We need to be patient. Heavenly Father knows best. Read D & C 97:8. The Lord knows our hearts and spirits.

Closing Prayer   Quickly read the lesson for next week.

Feeding the Five Thousand

Purpose: To teach of the miracles Jesus performed.

Supplies: Swedish fish (gummy fish)   Rolls or sliced bread
2 Baskets or 2 Towels   Scriptures
(matching or as similar as possible)

Advance Preparation: In a basket or towel, place two fish and five rolls or slices of bread. In the other basket or towel, place lots of fish and bread. (For economy, cut the rolls or bread into small pieces.) Take the second basket or towel and hide it where FHE will be held. Make sure it is hidden out of sight yet still readily available.

Opening Prayer

Song: Tell Me the Stories of Jesus   pg. 57 Children's Songbook

Activity: Turn to John 6 in the scriptures. Jesus had been preaching and performing miracles. A multitude (large group) of people had gathered to hear his words and be healed. Jesus asked his disciples how they would feed all these people with only five barley loaves and two fishes (vs. 2-9).

(Interesting point: Jesus all ready knew what he would do. This was an opportunity to prove who he was and what he had the power to do (vs. 6)).

Take the basket or towel with the five loaves and two fishes and place it before the family. Allow everyone to peak inside. It isn't very much food and it certainly won't feed a multitude. Read vs. 11-13. Jesus gave thanks for the food and shared it with the people. Everyone ate all they wanted and there was fish and bread left over. Jesus had performed a miracle.

Have someone say a prayer of thanks over the basket/towel. While everyone's eyes are closed switch the basket/towel for the hidden one. When the prayer is over, your family can experience what the multitude might have felt when they witnessed Jesus' miracle. Enjoy eating the fish and bread & share other miracles either scriptural or from your own lives.

Closing Prayer   Quickly read the lesson for next week.

Sacrament Reverence

Purpose: To focus on Jesus Christ during the administering of the Sacrament.

Supplies: Pictures of Jesus (clipart, Ensign/Friend clippings, etc.)
Paper   Glue/tape
Stapler   Scriptures
Markers, crayons, colored pencils, etc

Opening Prayer

Song: To Think about Jesus   pg. 71 Children's Songbook

Activity: Every Sunday we have the very special opportunity to renew our covenants with Heavenly Father and Jesus Christ. Covenants mean promises. By partaking of the bread and water of the Sacrament, we renew our promises.

During the Sacrament, we should be reverent and think of Jesus, the sacrifice he made for us, and the promises we have made with him. What are some of the promises we have made? Read D&C 20:77 and 79. We have promised to take upon ourselves the name of Jesus Christ, to always remember him, and to keep his commandments.

There are several things we can do to focus on Jesus Christ during the Sacrament. We can read the Sacrament prayers. We can also review the words to the Sacrament hymn. However, these ideas require reading skills. For younger children who cannot yet read, get some pictures of Jesus Christ. These pictures can be from any period of his life. Example: baby in a manger, preaching in the temple, calming the waters, etc. Take two pieces of paper and cut them into fourths. Put them together and staple them like a book. Allow the children to cut out the pictures of Jesus and glue/tape them to the pages of the book. The children can also color pictures of their family, Jesus, the temple, etc. on any blank pages. This "Sacrament Book" will help them to keep their focus and be reverent during the Sacrament.
Closing Prayer   Quickly read the lesson for next week.

Service Spotlight

Purpose: To teach the importance of service.

Supplies: Scriptures   Flashlight

Opening Prayer

Song: "Give," Said the Little Stream   pg. 236 Children's Songbook

Activity: Jesus taught the importance of service by example. He washed the feet of the disciples, healed the sick, lame, and blind. In the Book of Mormon days, there was a very good and wise man named King Benjamin. He taught that when we help our family, friends, neighbors, or even strangers, we are really helping God. Read aloud Mosiah 2:17.

Many times, Heavenly Father will answer someone's prayer and meet his/ her needs through other people. Those "other" people could be you or me. When we are prompted by the Holy Ghost to do something good for some- one, we should act on it. No matter how little or young we are, there are many ways for us to serve others. A few things we could do to help other people are: shine the Sunday shoes, pick up litter, help with the dishes, help someone with grocery bags, set up chairs in the Primary classroom, weed a garden, help entertain young children, walk the dog, tend animals, rake leaves, take in the mail, water the grass & flowers, etc. Add your own thoughts to make the list more complete and appropriate for the age of the children.

Now it is time not only to talk about service but to actually demonstrate it. Taking turns, allow each family member to select and demonstrate an act of service. The family may have to move to where the service will take place. Darken the room and shine the flashlight on the person performing the act of service. (A parent may need to control the flashlight if it is too distracting for the children.) Appreciate their actions with a round of applause, a cheer, and a pat on the back. Service is great! It makes both the person being helped and the person helping feel good.

We are thankful for the example of service Jesus was and for King Benjamin's teachings about service. When we are helping others we are serving Heavenly Father.

Challenge: Choose from the proceeding list something your family could do as a service project. Or create your own service project. Set a date to complete the service.

Closing Prayer

Quickly read the lesson for next week.

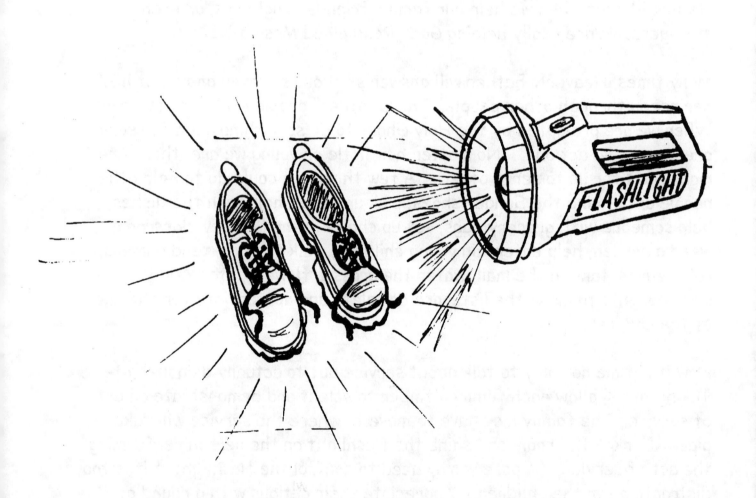

David & Goliath

Purpose: To emphasize that if we have faith and are obedient, the Lord will protect us.

Supplies: Large kitchen bowl   Wooden spoon
             Cookie Sheet   Scriptures
             Six men's socks

Opening Prayer

Song: Dare to Do Right   pg. 158 Children's Songbook

Activity: Long ago, there were two armies poised to fight. One army was the Philistines (bad guys) and the other was the army of Israel (good guys). Everyday a giant named Goliath challenged the Israelites. Read 1 Samuel 17:8-10. However, no soldier in the Israelite army was willing to fight Goliath for he was huge, strong, and an experienced fighter.

One day, a young boy named David was bringing food to his brothers in the Israelite army. He heard Goliath's challenge and was willing to fight him. David had faith in and was obedient to Heavenly Father. He knew the Lord would protect him. David went to King Saul to ask permission to fight Goliath. Read vs. 32-37.

King Saul gave his armor to David for protection but it was much too large. Instead, David was to face Goliath with only his faith as armor. David went to fight Goliath with his sling and five smooth stones. Read vs. 40. When Goliath saw small David, he said ... (read vs. 44-45). David then ran to fight Goliath. Read vs. 49. By using only a stone, his faith, and obedience, a young shepherd boy defeated a giant.

We have to face many giants today. Our giants may not be Philistine soldiers but rather pressure from friends to make wrong choices, watch inappropriate TV shows, swear, use drugs, etc. These things are just as dangerous to us as Goliath was to the Israelites. We must face our challenges as David did with faith in Heavenly Father and obedience to his commandments. Heavenly Father will protect us and help us through whatever trials we may face.

It was mentioned earlier that Goliath was a giant and that David was a young boy. It may be hard to understand what it was like to face someone so much larger and stronger. We are going to do a little role-playing that will demonstrate the difference. Have a parent, preferably the dad, put on the kitchen bowl as a helmet, use the wooden spoon as a sword, and the cookie sheet for a shield. Have one of the small children face him using one sock as a sling and five socks rolled up for stones. Remind the children that David fought Goliath with only five stones and a sling. Reenact the story of David and Goliath. Have some fun. Sling a few socks at dad. Point out the size difference to the children but explain that David was not frightened because he was righteous, knew he was doing what Heavenly Father wanted, and also knew the Lord would protect him.

Closing Prayer

Quickly read the lesson for next week.

The Liahona

Purpose: Develop increased faith.

Supplies: Compass   (or paper plate, brad, & paper arrow)
                Scriptures

Advance Preparation: If you do not have a compass, make one using the paper plate, brad, & paper arrow. Mark the plate with N, S, E and W. Hide several objects of your choice such as a ball, the scriptures, perhaps a sweet treat, etc.

Opening Prayer

Song: Faith   pg. 96 Children's Songbook

Activity: (Scriptural reference: Alma 37:35-46) After leaving Jerusalem, Lehi's family was camped in the wilderness at a place called the Valley of Lemuel. Lehi's sons returned to Jerusalem briefly to ask Ishmael and his family to join them. Upon their return, Lehi eagerly waited for instructions from the Lord. The Lord spoke to Lehi during the night, and commanded him to continue their journey. The next morning, at the door of his tent, Lehi found a round ball of curious workmanship. It acted as a compass, and it pointed the way Lehi's group should go. There were times the Liahona helped them. The Liahona directed Nephi where to go to hunt for food. Sometimes words appeared on the ball. From time to time the teachings and instructions appearing on the ball would change. These teachings and instructions were from the Lord. Lehi and his family learned that the Liahona would only guide them if they were faithful. If they became disobedient or murmured against the Lord, the Liahona ceased to work. When they repented and were faithful, the Liahona would direct them again. They were thankful for this gift and they tried to remain faithful so that they could enjoy this great blessing.

Now use the compass to find the things previously hidden.

Challenge: Live your life in such a way that the Lord could instruct you just as he did Lehi and his family. Practice obedience to a particular commandment of your choice. For example, try to complain less, pray for increased faith, etc.

Closing Prayer

Quickly read the lesson for next week.

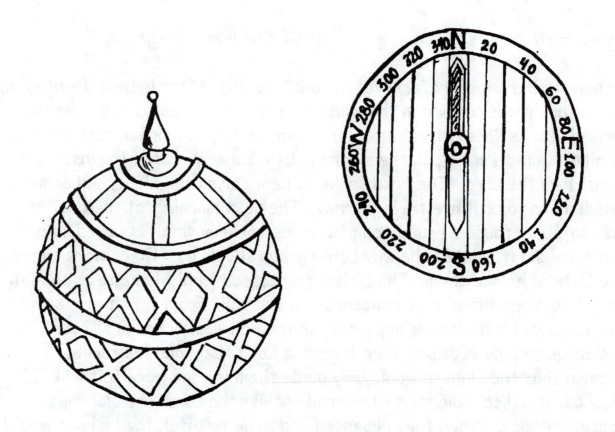

Noah's Ark

Purpose: Familiarization with the story of Noah and the Ark.

Supplies: Paper   Pencils   Scriptures

Opening Prayer

Song: Keep the Commandments   pg. 146 Children's Songbook

Activity: Open the scriptures to Genesis 6. Long ago, the people who lived on the earth were very disobedient. They did not follow the words of Heavenly Father and Jesus Christ. They were so wicked that the Lord decided to destroy man and the animals on the earth. Read vs. 7. However, Noah was a good man. He and his family obeyed the Lord.

Noah was commanded to build an ark. Read verses 14-16. Noah followed these instructions exactly. The Bible Dictionary indicates that a cubit is 17 ° to 21 ° inches in length. What a huge boat Noah built!

Noah was also commanded to gather two of every animal upon the earth, one male and the other female. Read verses 19-21. Food for the animals and for Noah's family was also stored in the huge ark.

The rains came. Noah loaded the animals two by two. Read Genesis 7:8-10. It rained for 40 days and nights. Read vs. 17-18. Noah, his family, and the animals drifted upon the water for over 150 days (vs. 24) before the waters dried and land was sighted. Noah and his family were saved from the flood because they were righteous and obedient.

Just as Noah was saved because of his righteousness, we can be saved if we are righteous. We must always listen to the Prophet, obey the commandments, and follow Jesus Christ's example. If we do, Heavenly Father will watch over, protect, and bless us.

We talked earlier about all the animals that were brought into the ark to be saved from the flood. Let's play a game similar to Pictionary involving all those animals. Have one person choose any kind of animal (don't tell what it is) and give him/her 20 seconds to draw it. The rest of the family

60

tries to guess it. Everyone take turns drawing. Add a fun spin by turning off the lights during the drawing time. Enjoy playing and being together as a family. Perhaps this is one of the games that Noah and his family played while they were in the ark.

Closing Prayer

Quickly read the lesson for next week.

Family Shield

Purpose: To emphasize the importance of having the Spirit in our homes.

Supplies:
Medium size bowl	Food coloring
3-4 Zip lock baggies	Pencils/pens
Piece of paper (8 ° x 11 inch paper divided into fourths)	
Scriptures	Old newspaper or paper towel

Opening Prayer

Song: Love Is Spoken Here   pg. 190 Children's Songbook

Activity: Today's world is wild and crazy. Satan is trying very hard to make sure we do not return to Heavenly Father. We have a place where we can go to be safe from Satan's influences. What is that place? (Our home) Our home is a sanctuary. A sanctuary is a place of peace where we feel safe. Why do we feel safe in our home? What is in our home that comforts us? It is the Spirit of the Lord. How is it that Heavenly Father and Jesus Christ can be in our home? They are invited into our homes by our actions and deeds. For example: praying, studying the scriptures, sharing, being gentle, and loving one another. Also it is important that we keep our homes clean and tidy. Read D & C 90:18. Heavenly Father and Jesus Christ cannot dwell in unclean or messy surroundings.

The Spirit that dwells in our home acts as a shield to protect our home from the influences of Satan. It is very important that we strengthen this shield and thus constantly invite the Spirit of Heavenly Father and Jesus Christ.

We are going to demonstrate the importance of this shield over our homes. Place the newspaper or paper towels on the table to prevent spill problems. Take the bowl and fill it half full with water. The food coloring and water represent Satan's influences. Add the food coloring drop by drop having each family member name one of Satan's influences. For example: back talking, swear words, inappropriate TV shows and computer games, lying, etc. Add enough food coloring that the water is quite dark. Now give a piece of paper and pencil/pen to everyone and have them draw

62

a little stick figure of him/herself. When done, place them in a baggie. The baggie represents the shield that is around our home. Now take that baggie and put it inside another baggie. This represents strengthening our shield. Continue to add baggies having each family member name something that strengthens the shield and invites the Spirit. For example: a clean and organized home, regular family home evenings, daily prayer and scripture study, no arguing and fighting, etc. Now the family is well protected by a strong shield. Have the family withstand Satan's influences. Demonstrate that the family can withstand Satan's influences by placing the baggie in the water, poking it down a bit if it tends to float, and leaving it for about 30 seconds. Remove the family from Satan's influence by taking the baggie out of the water. Remove the baggies one at a time. There is a chance that a little of Satan's influence (water) seeped through. That is why we must always build our shield stronger and stronger. Remove the last baggie and find that the family is safe and secure (dry) from Satan's influences because of the shield, the Spirit of Heavenly Father and Jesus Christ, around their home.

Satan wants to destroy the family. He is trying very hard to do so. We have a sanctuary. It is our home. It is the Spirit of Heavenly Father and Jesus Christ in our home that gives us peace and safety. We must always invite the Spirit in our homes and live so that the Spirit will remain.

Closing Prayer   Quickly read the lesson for next week.

New Year Time Capsule

Purpose: Documentation for our posterity.

Supplies: Paper
            Pencils/pens/markers
            Large manila envelope
            Family pictures

Opening Prayer

Song: Genealogy – I Am Doing It   pg. 94 Children's Songbook

Activity: Begin the year anew by remembering the past. Give each person in the family a piece of paper. Have everyone list his/her favorite song, book, TV show, subject in school, friend, hobby, color, movie, hopes, dreams, etc. Young children can draw a picture. On the back, parents should write what the drawing is about along with the child's name and age.

Gather the drawings, the lists of favorites, and a family picture. Place everything in the envelope. Write the date on the envelope and put it someplace safe. It can be opened and cherished at a future date.

The records we keep now will be very important to the family members that come after us. They will enjoy getting to know us and will learn from our experiences. "And we had obtained the records which the Lord had commanded us, and searched them and found that they were desirable; yea, even of great worth unto us. . ." (1 Nephi 5:21)

Closing Prayer

Quickly read the lesson for next week.

Valentine's Day

Purpose: To emphasize love of the Lord, others, and ourselves.

Supplies: Scriptures   Valentine candy (optional)
Picture of Jesus Christ with children (optional)

Opening Prayer

Song: Love One Another   pg. 136 Children's Songbook

Activity: Valentine's Day is a wonderful day. We scurry to give valentines to our family and friends to show how much we care about them.

Actually, to love one another is a commandment from Heavenly Father. Read Matthew 22:36-39. We should love Heavenly Father. And we should love others. Jesus Christ, our elder brother, was a wonderful example. He loved all people especially children. (If available, show the picture of Jesus.)

It is also very important to love ourselves. This is not an easy thing to do for we know ourselves better than anybody else. We often focus on our flaws and mistakes. Heavenly Father does not want us to do that. He loves us and we need to learn to love ourselves. Focus on your accomplishments and be proud of your name. Have each family member name one or two things he/she has accomplished which makes him/her feel good about him/herself. It may be something that seems small such as learning to tie a shoe, but actually all achievements are great.

Remember that we are all children of Heavenly Father and should feel good about who we are. When we truly love ourselves, we will be better able to love others and Heavenly Father.

(Optional: share the Valentine candy and continue to enjoy family achievements.)

Closing Prayer

Quickly read the lesson for next week.

Easter

Purpose: Review Christ's sacrifice for us and emphasize his resurrection.

Supplies: Scriptures   Empty box with lid   Empty glass
              Empty plastic egg   Empty envelope   Anything empty

Opening Prayer

Song: Jesus Has Risen   pg. 70 Children's Songbook

Activity: Review Christ's crucifixion by reading Luke 23:33-46. Quite often today's world associates Easter only with the death of Jesus Christ. That is why we see the cross. However, as members of the Church of Jesus Christ of Latter-Day Saints, we focus on the resurrection of Christ.

Jesus did not stay dead. Read Luke 24:6-7. The angels were announcing Christ's resurrection to Mary Magdalene, Joanna, and Mary at the now empty sepulcher. Later, Jesus appeared to the apostles and said. . . read Luke 24:36-39.

Take the gathered objects and place them before the family. Ask the family what these things have to do with Easter. Let them open the box, envelope, egg, etc. If necessary, give the hint that these things are similar to Christ's tomb. All these things are empty just as Christ's tomb was empty. Jesus was not there. He was resurrected. Jesus had a body of flesh and bones and was teaching people about the Gospel.

Easter is about the crucifixion, resurrection, teachings, and example of Jesus Christ. Jesus taught to believe in him, repent, keep the commandments and follow his example. If we do all of these things, because of his sacrifice, we will be able to have eternal life with our Heavenly Father and Jesus Christ.

Closing Prayer

Quickly read the lesson the next week.

Mother's/Father's Day

Purpose: To appreciate what our Mothers and Fathers teach us.

Supplies: For Mother's Day, gather mom's shoes, apron, dress, etc. For Father's Day, gather dad's boots, shirt, tie, belt, etc. Scriptures

Opening Prayer

Song: A Happy Family   pg. 198 Children's Songbook

Activity: We are so blessed to be a family. Heavenly Father wants families to return to live with him. We have much to learn to be ready and worthy to go back to Heavenly Father. The Lord has helpers which are Moms (say Dads for Father's Day). They have so much to teach. Moms (Dads) help with the very basics such as walking and talking. They also help with very difficult things such as school subjects. They teach us to work to learn responsibility. Our Moms (Dads) teach us the principles of the Gospel. Have every family member share something he/she has learned from Mom (Dad).

The teaching done by Mom (Dad) and the learning done by the children are very serious matters to Heavenly Father. Read Exodus 20:12. "Honoring" means "obeying" and is one of the Ten Commandments.

We have much to learn and do so that we may be ready and worthy to return to our Heavenly Father. He has given us Moms (Dads) to teach us and to be an example for us. We must learn our lessons well.

It has been said that imitation is the sincerest form of flattery. Here is the chance to really flatter Mom (Dad). Using the gathered items, dress-up like Mom (Dad) and act out something. Examples: Mom doing dishes, Mom playing the piano or crocheting, Dad tinkering with power tools, Dad reading the paper, etc. Another fun activity is to have dress-up races. Time each person as he/she dresses in the gathered items. Fastest time wins.

Closing Prayer   Quickly read the lesson for next week.

4th of July

Purpose: To appreciate the sacrifices made by our ancestors for our freedom. And to recognize the Lord's hand in the fight for independence.

Supplies: Scriptures   Paper   Crayons/Markers
              Pillow cases (one per family member)   Blocks

Opening Prayer

Song: My Country 'Tis of Thee

Activity: America is a very special land. Heavenly Father began preparing this land long ago. America is where he brought the Jaredites and Lehi and his family. The Land of Promise mentioned in the Book of Mormon is the American continent. Heavenly Father also guided Columbus, the discoverer of this land. Heavenly Father then helped to establish our government by guiding the men who wrote the constitution. Read D & C 101:80. He wants this land to be strong, free, and faithful.

Only July 4th 1776, our nation became free. It was not easy. A long, hard war was fought and many people died. Because of their sacrifice, we have many blessings and opportunities today. Have every family member name a freedom we have today. For example: we choose our own profession, where we live, who our leaders are, etc.

It is our responsibility to keep this country free. We should vote (when eligible), proudly say the Pledge of Allegiance, properly display the flag, be a good example, help our fellow neighbor, pray for our leaders, and more. Heavenly Father prepared this land long ago. We must keep it great.

Have a little fun with family battles. Every person will be his/her own country. Give everyone a piece of paper and crayon/marker. Have everyone name his/her country and design a flag. Next, battle it out over thumb wars (lock hands and try to pin the other person's thumb down with your thumb), block stacking (highest stack before falling down wins), and pillow case races (just like gunny sack races). Winners battle winners until there is one ultimate winner. Have fun.

Closing Prayer   Quickly read the lesson for next week.

Halloween

Purpose: To review the rules for Halloween fun.

Supplies: Bowl of Halloween candy

Opening Prayer

Song: If You're Happy   pg. 268 Children's Songbook

Activity: Halloween is a very fun time of the year. We have the chance to use our imagination and create wonderful costumes. We can be a clown, a pirate, a doctor, an astronaut, or anything else. Have each member of the family say something he/she would like to dress up as.

It is so fun to dress up and pretend that we are something else for an evening; but we must always remember who we truly are. We are sons and daughters of Heavenly Father. And we must act in an appropriate way. Heavenly Father would not want us to play mean tricks such as toilet papering houses, throwing rocks or eggs, soaping windows, etc. Nor does he want us to scare little children.

Heavenly Father would like us to use our manners. Remember to say thank you when given candy. If a bowl of candy is placed before you, take only one or two pieces. Share with other family members.

Also, Heavenly Father wants us to be safe. "...The beloved of the Lord shall dwell in safety..." (Deuteronomy 33:12) Only Trick-or-Treat to people that you know. Stay in well lit areas. Go with a parent or friend. Look both ways when crossing the street. Let Mom and Dad examine the candy before you eat it.

Remember, we are sons and daughters of Heavenly Father and we must act that way. He wants us to have fun but he also wants us to be nice, polite, and safe. Use your imagination and enjoy the evening.

Take a few minutes to practice Trick-or-Treating. Practice saying thank you and taking only one or two pieces of candy from a bowl. Talk about which neighbors you will be visiting on Halloween.

Closing Prayer   Quickly read the lesson for next week.

Thanksgiving

Purpose: To be thankful for blessings and to show thankfulness by giving.

Supplies: Scriptures Hymnbook Children's Songbook
Paper Pen/Pencil/Markers Can or Cans of Soup

Opening Prayer

Song: Count Your Blessings pg. 241 Hymnbook

Activity: Today we are going to talk about being thankful. Look under "thankfulness" and "gratitude" in the Bible dictionary and topical guide. There are many words linked to them. Have each family member say one of the words (praise, rejoice, indebted, bless) or one they think of. We have been so BLESSED by the Lord. We are eternally INDEBTED to him. We should PRAISE him and REJOICE for all that he has given us.

Now, look in the Hymnbook and Children's Songbook under the same topics. There are many songs. Give each family member the opportunity to point out a song. Perhaps it is his/her favorite.

Why do you think there are so many words and songs relating to thankfulness? (Give time to answer.) We are all blessed beyond measure. Heavenly Father has given us a family who loves us, the Church to guide us, a Prophet to lead us, a warm house to live in, food to eat, and so much more. We must recognize his hand and give thanks in all things. We should even be thankful for trials because we will learn from them and become better people as a result. Have each family member name something to be thankful for.

It is very important to be thankful for all of our many blessings. We should show our thankfulness to the Lord. Read D & C 42:38. One way we can show our thankfulness to Heavenly Father for all that we have been given is by giving unto others. We can give in ways such as taking cookies to a neighbor, raking leaves or shoveling the neighbor's walk, giving food to the food bank, donating blankets & toys to a homeless shelter, sharing our talents and time at a nursing home, being friendly and happy to all, etc.

71

Our family has been very blessed. We can show our thankfulness to the Lord by giving unto others. As a family, decide on something you can do for others that will show your gratitude to Heavenly Father.

In addition to being thankful to Heavenly Father, we should show our gratitude to other people. Often people do things for us and we forget to say thank you. For example: for children who went to school today, did you remember to say "thank you" to the bus driver, carpool driver, or parent who got you safely there? Did you say "thank you" to the lunch ladies or to mom for a scrumptious meal? We need to be more aware of people and the work they do for us.

Thank you cards are a wonderful way to express gratitude. Christmas will soon be here. When we receive gifts for Christmas, thank you cards are both appropriate and appreciated. We also need to remember to express appreciation for birthday gifts and for any gifts we receive throughout the year.

Take a moment to think of someone that has helped you recently. Perhaps this someone has helped the entire family. Or each family member could think of different people for whom he/she would like to say "thank you." Take a can of soup. The flavor doesn't matter. Write a little note saying "Thanks! You are "Souper!" Younger children may enjoy coloring this note. Give this little gift of appreciation to someone deserving. It will make his/her day.

Closing Prayer

Quickly read the lesson for next week.

Christmas Gift

Purpose: To emphasize the true meaning of Christmas, which is to celebrate the birth of Christ.

Supplies: Nativity set   Box   Wrapping paper
              Tape   Scissors   Children's Songbook
              Scriptures

Advance Preparation: Wrap the nativity set in the box.

Opening Prayer

Song: Skip the song at this point. We will sing during the lesson.

Activity: This is a wonderful time of the year. Everyone is cheerful, the decorations are so pretty, and there are many wonderful gifts. We are going to open a gift early this year. This gift is fantastic and it will help us focus on what Christmas is truly about. Allow the children to open the gift and carefully remove the nativity set.

Christmas is the celebration of the birth of Jesus Christ. This nativity set is a recreation of that birth. (Turn to The Nativity Song pg. 52 Children's Songbook). We are going to talk about each piece of the nativity set and its role in Jesus' birth as we put it together. Sing all five verses of the Nativity Song and place each piece. Ask the children if they understand who or what each piece represents and if they have any questions about Christ's birth.

You may want to take this opportunity to quickly review the story of Christ's birth. Read Luke 2:1-20.

Jesus Christ is what Christmas is all about. We often focus on the gifts and goodies and forget who and what we are celebrating. Look at the nativity often and sing the song. Remember Jesus Christ.

Challenge: Remember Jesus Christ throughout the entire holiday season.

Closing Prayer   Quickly read the lesson for next week.

Christmas Music

Purpose: To understand the lyrics for traditional Christmas songs in order to bring the focus back on Jesus Christ.

Supplies: Hymnbook
            Children's Songbook
            Scriptures

Opening Prayer

Song: Skip this for now. You will be singing for the activity.

Activity: Read D & C 136:28. Music is a very important part of worship. It invites the spirit into our hearts. Unfortunately, often we sing songs without really knowing or paying attention to the words. Turn to the Christmas songs in the Hymnbook and Children's Songbook. Allow a family member to pick a favorite song. Sing and enjoy the song. Then go through the song verse by verse. Understand what the song is about. Explain anything that might be confusing to the children. Sing and review a song choice for each family member.

Christmas is all about the birth of Jesus Christ. Singing and understanding these beautiful songs will help us focus on that and keep the true spirit of the holiday season.

Challenge: Keep Jesus Christ as the focus of Christmas.

Closing Prayer

Quickly read the lesson for next week.